Francisco Pizarro

Discover The Life Of An Explorer

Trish Kline

Rourke

Publishing LLC

Vero Beach, Florida 32964

www.rourkepublishing.com

PHOTO CREDITS: IRC-www.historypictures.com: cover, title page, pages 4, 7, 12, 17, 18, 21; © Hulton/Archive by Getty Images: pages 8, 10, 15; © Artville: page 13.

Title page: Francisco Pizarro led a life of dangerous adventure.

Editor: Frank Sloan

Cover design by Nicola Stratford

Library of Congress Cataloging-in-Publication Data

Kline, Trish
    Francisco Pizarro / Trish Kline.
      p. cm. — (Discover the life of an explorer)
    Summary: Introduces the life of Francisco Pizarro, the explorer who was sent to Peru by the king of Spain to conquer the Incas and claim their land and wealth for the Spanish crown.
    Includes bibliographical references (p.)and index.
    ISBN 1-58952-297-4
    1. Pizarro, Francisco, ca. 1475-1541—Juvenile literature. 2. Peru—History—Conquest, 1522-1548—Juvenile literature. 3. Incas—Juvenile literature. 4. South America—Discovery and exploration—Spanish—Juvenile literature. 6. Explorers—Spain—Biography—Juvenile literature. [1. Pizarro, Francisco, ca. 1475-1541. 2. Peru—History—Conquest, 1522-1548. 3. Incas. 4. Indians of South America. 5. Explorers. 6. South America—Discovery and exploration—Spanish.] I. Title.

F3442.P776 K55 2002
985'.02'092—dc21
[B]
                                     2002020710

Printed in the USA
CG/CG

TABLE OF CONTENTS

SEEKING ADVENTURE

Francisco Pizarro (FRAHN see sko PETE zahr oh) was born in Spain around 1475. He was very poor. He never learned to read or write. His father was a captain in the army. Francisco did not want to be a soldier. He wanted to sail the seas.

In 1509, Pizarro set sail for adventures in the New World. His first **voyage** was on a ship bound for present-day Colombia. Then, in 1513, Pizarro sailed with **Vasco de Balboa**. On this voyage, Balboa first sighted the Pacific Ocean and claimed it for Spain.

Pizarro sailed with Balboa when Balboa discovered the Pacific Ocean.

GOLD!

Pizarro wanted to discover new lands. He wanted to claim the lands for the king of Spain. During the 1520s, Pizarro led two **expeditions**. These sailed along the west coast of South America. He had heard tales of a land rich in gold. This land was the present-day country of Peru.

Pizarro soon met Native Americans of the Inca tribe. The Inca lived in Peru. The Inca wore beautiful items made of gold.

The Inca decorated themselves with gold objects.

SENT TO CONQUER

Pizarro returned to Spain. He told the king about the Inca. He told the king that the Inca were dressed in gold. The king told Pizarro to **conquer** the land and its people. He promised Pizarro that he would be the ruler of Peru. The king also told Pizarro to take all of the gold. He was to claim it for Spain.

Pizarro told the Spanish king about Inca treasure.

INVITATION TO A FEAST

In 1532, Pizarro took an army and returned to Peru. When he arrived, he invited the chief of the Indians and his people to a feast. **Atahualpa,** the chief of the Inca, accepted. He and his men arrived at the feast without weapons. He thought Pizarro and the Spaniards wanted to be friends.

This was what Pizarro wanted the chief to think. It was a trick.

The Inca chief begged Pizarro for his life after learning of Pizarro's trick.

Pizarro's men took Atahualpa prisoner.

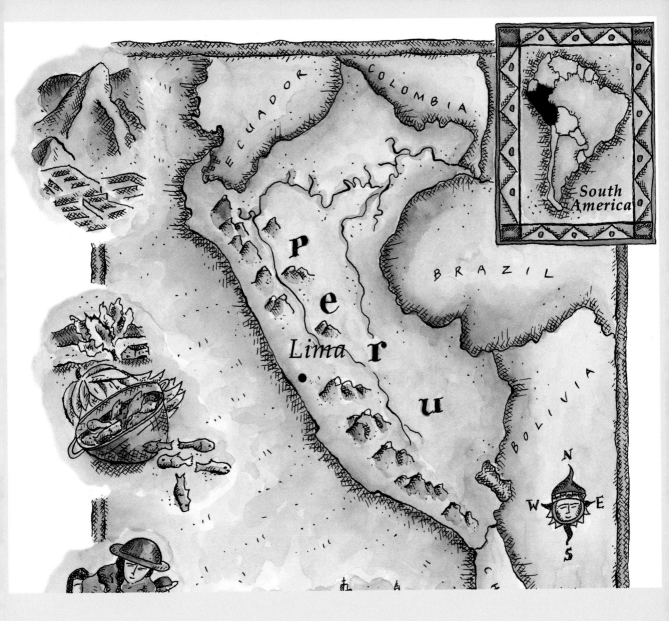

Pizarro discovered the Inca Empire in the mountains of Peru.

BROKEN PROMISE

Pizarro had his army surround the Inca. He made the chief his prisoner. Pizarro told his army to kill all of the Inca.

The chief told Pizarro of the tribe's great riches. He said he would give these to Pizarro if the Spaniard would spare his life. Pizarro promised he would let the chief live.

Atahualpa did as Pizarro asked, but Pizarro had him killed anyway.

Atahualpa filled a large room with gold. He filled two smaller rooms with silver. When the rooms were filled, the chief asked Pizarro to let him go.

However, Pizarro did not keep his promise. Instead, Pizarro had Atahualpa killed. The tribe was forced to be Pizarro's slaves.

Atahualpa gave Pizarro gifts of gold and silver.

WAR AND REVENGE

Pizarro had a palace built for himself in the city of Lima. In 1538, Pizarro and **Diego de Almagro,** another Spanish **explorer,** argued over who should rule a certain piece of land. This led to a war. Pizarro won. He captured Almagro and had him killed.

Soon, Almagro's son sought **revenge**. Pizarro was attacked in his palace. A band of people surprised him as he ate dinner. Though he tried to escape, he was killed.

Pizarro was attacked and killed in his palace in Lima.

RULER OF PERU

Pizarro ruled the land of Peru from 1532 to 1541. He founded the city of Lima, the present-day capital of Peru. He also explored several other countries in South America, including present-day Ecuador and Colombia.

Pizarro's body was laid to rest in Peru.

IMPORTANT DATES TO REMEMBER

1475	Born in Spain
1509	Set sail for the New World
1520s	Led expeditions in South America
1532	Returned to Peru where he defeated the Incas
1541	Died at age 66

GLOSSARY

Almagro, Diego de (ahl MAWG row, DEE egg oh duh) —
a Spanish explorer

Atahualpa (AH tuh WALL puh) — chief of the Inca

Balboa, Vasco de (BAL bow uh, VAS koh duh) —
a Spanish explorer

conquer (KONG ker) — to overcome by force

expeditions (EK spi dish enz) — journeys or trips made for
certain purposes like finding gold

explorer (ek SPLOR er) — someone who travels to
unknown places

revenge (ri VENJ) — action taken to get even or to return injury
for injury

voyage (VOY ij) — a trip to a faraway place

INDEX

Further Reading

De Angelis, Gina. *Francisco Pizarro and the Conquest of the Inca*. Chelsea House
    Publishing, 2000.
Manning, Ruth. *Francisco Pizarro*. Heinemann Library, 2001.

Websites To Visit

www.encarta.com
www.gale.com
www.pbs.org
www.mariner.org (The Mariner's Museum, Newport News, VA)

About The Author

Trish Kline has written a great number of nonfiction books for the school and library market. Her publishing credits include two dozen books, as well as hundreds of newspaper and magazine articles, anthologies, short stories, poetry, and plays. She lives in Helena, Montana.